1,000,000 Books
are available to read at

www.ForgottenBooks.com

Read online
Download PDF
Purchase in print

ISBN 978-1-330-74645-5
PIBN 10100027

This book is a reproduction of an important historical work. Forgotten Books uses state-of-the-art technology to digitally reconstruct the work, preserving the original format whilst repairing imperfections present in the aged copy. In rare cases, an imperfection in the original, such as a blemish or missing page, may be replicated in our edition. We do, however, repair the vast majority of imperfections successfully; any imperfections that remain are intentionally left to preserve the state of such historical works.

Forgotten Books is a registered trademark of FB &c Ltd.
Copyright © 2018 FB &c Ltd.
FB &c Ltd, Dalton House, 60 Windsor Avenue, London, SW19 2RR.
Company number 08720141. Registered in England and Wales.

For support please visit www.forgottenbooks.com

1 MONTH OF FREE READING

at
www.ForgottenBooks.com

By purchasing this book you are eligible for one month membership to ForgottenBooks.com, giving you unlimited access to our entire collection of over 1,000,000 titles via our web site and mobile apps.

To claim your free month visit:
www.forgottenbooks.com/free100027

* Offer is valid for 45 days from date of purchase. Terms and conditions apply.

English
Français
Deutsche
Italiano
Español
Português

www.forgottenbooks.com

Mythology Photography **Fiction**
Fishing Christianity **Art** Cooking
Essays Buddhism Freemasonry
Medicine **Biology** Music **Ancient Egypt** Evolution Carpentry Physics
Dance Geology **Mathematics** Fitness
Shakespeare **Folklore** Yoga Marketing
Confidence Immortality Biographies
Poetry **Psychology** Witchcraft
Electronics Chemistry History **Law**
Accounting **Philosophy** Anthropology
Alchemy Drama Quantum Mechanics
Atheism Sexual Health **Ancient History**
Entrepreneurship Languages Sport
Paleontology Needlework Islam
Metaphysics Investment Archaeology
Parenting Statistics Criminology
Motivational

MARINA,

AND

OTHER POEMS.

BY

BOSCAWEN TREVOR GRIFFITH.

LONDON:
WHITTAKER AND CO.;
CHESTER; CATHERALL & PRICHARD, EASTGATE ROW.
MDCCCLIX.

CATHERALL AND PRICHARD, PRINTERS,
CHESTER.

PR
4728
G835m

MARINA,
AND OTHER POEMS.

CONTENTS.

Marina, a Tale of Capri	1
A Lament for Rome	23
The Eve of the Attack	31
An Episode of War	35
Queen Victoria's Farewell to the Baltic Fleet	41
The Vale of Rydal	43
Sonnets, I. Disappointment	48
,, II. Hope	49
,, III. Melancholy	50
,, IV. Contentment	51
,, V. Mystery	52
,, VI. Affection	53
Song	54
Constancy	55
To a Young Lady on her Birthday	56
Song "Those eyes of Thine"	57
Ode to "The Derby"	59
The Novel and the Stage	65

THE following Poems are presented to the Public with a full knowledge of the very trifling merit which they possess. Being a selection from a somewhat large number of pieces, written from time to time at the author's leisure, they are necessarily of a miscellaneous character; and for a few of them, composed at an early age, some especial indulgence must be solicited.

TREVALYN HALL.
February 1859.

MARINA;

A TALE OF CAPRI.

" Quum procul obscuros colles, humilemque videmus
  Italiam *   *   *   *   *   *   *
  Italiam lœto socii clamore salutant."
                                    VIRGIL, *Æn. III.*
" Illa dies fatum miseræ mihi dixit : ab illâ
  Pessima mutati cæpit amoris hyems."
                                    OVID, *Heroid, Ep.* v.

THE sky is bright, the billow's breast
Calm as an unweaned babe at rest,
And scarce a sound or motion there
Disturbs the silence of the air;
Where, on the deep blue tinted wave
That doth those southern regions lave,
The listless barque awaits, unmoved,
A fav'ring breeze that false has proved;
The land, far distant on the lee,
Across a broad expanse of sea,
Might to the sailor's vision seem
Some dim creation of a dream,

So faintly, half in mist effaced,
The outline on th' horizon traced,
Where constant strain the wand'rer's eyes—
'T is Italy before them lies!

'T is Italy! thou hallow'd ground!
What glories in thy name abound!
Since 'scaped from Grecian sword and flame,*
A fleet of exiled warriors came,
Their fortunes on thy soil to trace,
The germ of Rome's undying race.
Fallen thou art; but no decay
Can sweep thy grandeur all away;
The fame that deathless to thee clings,
Yet o'er thy plains illusion flings;
The faded splendour of the past,
Spark of a flame too bright to last.

Behold that soft bewitching Bay,
The fount of many a poet's lay,
Parthenope's enchanted shore,
The nurse, the grave of classic lore;

---

* Alluding to the supposed colonization of Italy by the Trojans; the greater portion, however, of the present kingdom of Naples was occupied by Greek colonies, and hence often called "Magna Grecia."

Sweet land! the loved Campanian home,
The soft retreat of mighty Rome.*

  * * * * * * *

There is an islet dark and blue,
From Naples' sunny shore in view,
Cradled upon the dancing waves
Which sport amid her rocky caves,
Shedding their azure image bright,
Reflected in the clear sunlight,
O'er the deep vaults that pierce unseen
Her cliff-bound sides the rocks between.
'Tis Capri! nature's wayward child,
So strangely fanciful, so wild:
Whose rocky solitude delights
To scorn Sorrento's softer heights;
And yet the fragments† on her hill
Of ancient pomp no heart can fill

---

* The supposed tomb of Virgil is still shewn at Posilipo, near Naples. This neighbourhood was a favourite resort of many of the Roman nobles, as well as of Pliny, Cicero, Virgil, and other great poets and writers.

† Capri was the scene of the infamous excesses which disgraced the last years of the Emperor Tiberius. The ruins of the twelve palaces, erected by him to the twelve superior divinities, are now little more than shapeless heaps, the palaces having been destroyed at the Emperor's death by order of the Senate.

With pleasing thought, the base retreat
Of infamy, of deeds more meet
For lowest hell, of tyrant rage,
They stand accursed in hist'ry's page.—
But see, again the breezy air
Deigns on her course the barque to bear,
Fills out the canvass; from the prow
The silvery foam leaps glitt'ring now:
The crew, uproused, trim every sail
To woo the gently rising gale;
The steersman grasps his helm anew,
His eye is on that islet blue.
Fast speeds the boat, now on the beach,
Long ere she can the island reach,
Rude fishermen may be descried,
While from the mountain, side by side,
To hail the wanderers, dark-eyed maids,
Their tresses bound in classic braids*
Descend, with loving lips to greet,
And welcomes, to the sailor sweet,

---

* In many of the cities of Greek origin, the hair of the women is still worn coiled round their heads in the manner of ancient sculpture.

A brother some, and some a lover,
Nor strive these last their joy to cover;
Nature to them is all in all,
Nought in the wide world can they call
Their portion, save the priceless wealth
Of youth, content, and joyous health.

On the shore of the islet there stands one alone,
   Alone mid'st a crowd is he;
His visage is dark, with a heart heavy grown,
   Doth he gaze on the far-spreading sea.

But yet, as his eye on that fast-nearing barque
   Alights for a moment, there beams
A swift fading smile on his countenance dark,
   As a ray of the sun through a wilderness gleams.

In a safe little creek now the vessel is moored,
   And swift through the surf spring the sailors to shore;
With welcome and laughter they soon are assured
   Of the constancy sworn by their sweethearts of yore.

The lonely one turned from the scene, and away
   To a rock far removed he sped,—
"Ah!" cried he, aloud, "'t is a year to the day
   " Since I came, too, from sea to be wed!

" Oh! happy, light-hearted, and joyous was I,
   " Then leaping ashore from the main;
" And to greet me a true maiden's bright-flashing eye
   " Gave the joy I can ne'er feel again,

" Marina! my love, my affianced, my wife,
   " Mine no more! and, denied to my hate,
" The betrayer who drained the delight from my life
   " Derides yet the justice of fate."

With visage averted he bent to the earth,
   While still the breeze bore to his ear
The echoes of revelry, laughter, and mirth,
   Which awaken'd the beach far and near.

For a time, half unconscious, in sorrow he lay,
   Till sudden the dark manly face,
The features of one whom he thought far away,
   He seemed as if dreaming to trace:

'T is Antonio, his comrade, the self-same attire,
  The fisherman's dress that he wore;
Ah! what mem'ries of old did that vision inspire
  Of friendship, and pleasures no more!

    Started the mourner to his feet,
  " Antonio, do we once more meet?
  " Companion of my joyous youth,
  " Long proved in friendship and in truth,
  " What dost thou here in Capri's isle?
  " On thee the joys of fortune smile;
  " Blest in thy home, Salerno's shore
  " Can charm thy wedded spirit more
  " Than this lone crag." Thus Giulio cried,
    And thus the fisherman replied:
  " Giulio, thy wrongs are heard, are known
  " To thine Antonio; why alone
  " Thou sitt'st in grief, nor join'st the throng
  " Of revellers, the dance and song.
  " As in Salerno's bay my boat,
  " On the blue waves once more afloat,
  " Last evening flew before the wind,
  " And left Amalfi far behind,

" A little barque my prow there crossed
" Gaily upon the billows tossed ;
" I knew her rig, her island build,
" Longings for thee my bosom filled,—
" I hailed her ; at her rudder stood
" Francesco, thine old playmate ; Could
" He tell me how my Giulio fared ?
" I asked. The youth a moment stared,
" As if in doubt, then sudden leapt
" Within my boat ; his comrade kept
" Their vessel on our beam, while he
" Ran quickly o'er the tale to me :
" How Fra Gennaro had profaned
" Thy heart's best love, how nought remained
" But vengeance. Giulio, thine of yore
" To save my sister,—though no more
" Alas ! she loves thee ; yet, behold,
" Not so Antonio's love grown cold ;
" I will avenge thee ! Mine the blow
" To lay the foul seducer low ;
" Fearless his footsteps to pursue,
" Till his life-blood this hand bedew."

He ceased; and as the words yet rang
In Giulio's ear, Antonio sprang
Swift as the Alpine chamois bounds
From rock to rock, the dying sounds
Were barely hushed, ere, blithe anew,
He joined again the merry crew;—
In revelry the evening sped,
With laughter crowned, till darkness spread
Her shadows, from the azure height
Shone forth the moon,—the summer night
Blazed with the starry host of heaven;
Then, kisses to each maiden given,
Farewell to all; loth to remain,
Antonio seeks his boat again.
The dripping oars the moonbeams gild,
Anon, the loosened sail is filled,
And in the dim uncertain light
The *barca* wings her rapid flight
Forth from the island, far away,
O'er slumb'ring Naples' silent bay.

Brightly beams the sunny morning,
    Bella Napoli, on thee,
Rosy tints thy gems adorning,
    Peerless princess of the sea.

Mark the sombre smoke ascending
    From Vesuvius' lofty heights,
Strangely in the landscape blending
    Nature's terrors and delights.

To the mountain's dark slopes clinging,
    Town and village clustered lie,
Though each fleeting day be bringing
    Dread destruction yet more nigh.

Yet, light-hearted, gay as ever,
    Still the peasants laugh and love ;
Building, planting, dreaming never
    Of the storm that lowers above !

Where of old a city, falling
    In the lava's headlong course,
Met a fate the world appalling,
    Buried 'neath the torrent's force ;

Now, with happiness beguiling
    To forget its ancient doom,
Bright Castellamare smiling
    Rears herself on Stabiœ's* tomb.

Here, as if seclusion wooing,
    In a little bay she lies,
E'er the cooling breeze renewing,
    Naples' heated shore denies.

Round her brow the vines entwining,
    Like a verdant chaplet meet,
While the azure waters, shining
    In the sunbeams, lave her feet.

Here, at the early dawn of day,
A little barque at anchor lay:
And, while Castellamare slept,
In silence hushed, Antonio leapt

---

* Castellamare, a small town in an angle of the Bay of Naples, and a favourite resort of the Neapolitans during the heat of summer, is built upon the ruins of the ancient Stabiœ, which city was overwhelmed by the same eruption which entombed Herculaneum and Pompeii, A.D. 79.

Forth to the land, and quickly sped
Through street on street; while from his bed
'Neath some dark porch, the beggar rose,
And sought in vain to interpose
A muttered prayer for alms; unheard,
Unheeded fell each piteous word;
Ceaseless the fisherman pursued
His onward path, as if endued
With strength untiring, till awhile
He paused unmoved, and then a smile,
A fearful smile, o'erspread his face,
When, from a lonely dwelling place,
A woman's joyous accents rang,
As if a merry song she sang
To one who loved her; " he is there,"
Antonio muttered, " Ah! beware,
" False monk! just vengeance waits at last
" Thy steps, atonement for the past
" Nought but thy blood can buy! 't is mine
" To crush that craven heart of thine!"—
An hour has fled; Antonio still,
Eager his mission to fulfil,
Low crouches there, while at delay
His spirit chafes; the breaking day

Grows brighter, soon the slumb'ring town
Will rise to life, and failure crown
His firm-fix'd purpose : at the thought
He shuddered ; had he vainly sought
His holy vengeance ? List ! a sound
Comes faintly to his ear ; around
The sea, the houses seem to melt ;
The portal opes,—forth from his belt
He draws his weapon ; slow emerge
Two forms, yet one, a friar's serge
Who wears, but meets his anxious eye ;—
A loud report, one piercing cry
Of mortal agony appalls
The murd'rer's ear, and prostrate falls
A lovely woman bathed in blood !
Deprived of sense, Antonio stood
A moment in amazement lost ;
Then high in air away he tossed
The erring pistol, forth he drew
His sailors knife, and rushed anew
On the pale monk, who, filled with dread,
Low bent beside the beauteous dead,—
One desp'rate lunge Antonio made,
And buried his avenging blade

Deep in the dark betrayer's heart;
And, as the red drops spouting start,
He plucked the weapon back, and cried,
" Giulio, thou art avenged ! " then hied
Swift from the scene of blood away,
Unmoored his boat, and, 'ere the day
By one brief hour hath older grown,
Far o'er the bay his sail hath flown !—
Still ever ringing in his ear
Marina's death-cry shrill and clear,
In vain from land the breezes bore
Antonio dyed with reeking gore;
Holy Madonna! dearly bought
The vengeance he had rashly sought,
Bought with the blood of Giulio's bride,
Faithless, yet fondly loved she died,
" Slain by this erring hand," he cried ;
" Oh ! Giulio, mine the hapless fate
" In purest friendship, to create
" For thee thy crowning woe ! thine heart,
" Oh, must it with its idol part,
" Lov'd from its childhood ? though betrayed,
" Ne'er while she breathed, its hope could fade."

Two days have fled—of what befell
In that brief space, suffice to tell
How, hurried back across the bay,
By justice seized, Antonio lay
In Naples' dungeons dark and cold,
Waiting his doom :—to Giulio told
Marina's death, his home he left,
Like one of sense and reason reft ;—
Vain o'er the Isle the peasants sought
His wander'd track ; for ever fraught
With mystery his secret fate ;
Yet oft one fisher would relate
A tale of Giulio that he dreamed,
And thus to him the vision seemed :—

'Neath a high cliff on Capri's strand,
Guided as by a Nereid's wand,
The dark blue torrents rapid sweep
Within an entrance low and deep,
And there the restless heaving wave
Hath hewn itself a lofty cave ;—
A wand'red sunbeam, thither strayed,
A fairy hall the cavern made ;

Too near the rocky arch once glancing,
A billow, tow'rds the grotto dancing,
Bore it within ;—imprisoned fast,
Above, around, its lustre cast
The impress of the azure sky,
Snatched from the glorious world on high ;
A wondrous paradise ! to show
How to the lowliest spot below,
Heaven with its glory can descend,
A portion of its light to lend,
And to the darkest humblest heart
A ray of hope and joy impart.

To this fair spot in brightest blue
At early morning bathed anew,
Giulio had pierced, for oft of old,
Its matchless wonders to behold,
'T was his delight within to float,
Borne on a little tossing boat ;—
In joy its fairy grandeur charmed
His heart, its solemn silence calmed
In woe his turbid soul, and now,
With swimming head, and aching brow,

O'erwhelmed with grief, with burning thought
Oppressed, once more alone he sought
The azure grotto ;*—solitude
Meet for the mourner's heart, to brood
On vanished hopes, on joys decayed,
On life a living torture made.

" Ripples round the rocky walls,
 " Softly murmuring, the sea,
" With a music that recalls
 " Days of happiness to me.

" So in hours of pleasure flown,
 " Did'st thou chaunt thy tender lay,
" When thy winning smile alone,
 " All my cares could charm away.

* The Grotta Azzurra, here referred to, is a large cavern on the coast of Capri, which can only be entered in a small boat made for the purpose. The whole of the interior is of a most beautiful ultramarine colour, caused by the refraction of the rays of the sun, which penetrate the narrow mouth of the Grotto.

D

" When thou breath'dst within mine ear
  " Holy vows that live on high,
" Yet without one pitying tear,
  " Could'st thou from my bosom fly!

" Though upon the restless sea
  " Daily 't was my lot to roam,
" Wandered ere my heart from thee,
  " Cherished treasure of my home?

" Till the tempter's treach'rous lure,
  " 'Neath confession's seal, instilled
" Poison in thy spirit pure,
  " And thy life with darkness filled.

" O Marina, liv'st thou yet?
  " To my longing arms return,—
' All my wrongs I would forget,
  " And for thee forgiveness learn!

" Dead! oh, no, it cannot be,
  " In my ear her voice is ringing,
" Still imploring pardon, see
  " To my knees Marina clinging.

"Yes, I go to her embrace,
  "All our former love renew,
"Where her silv'ry* form I trace,
  "Deep beneath the vault of blue.

"Beauteous grotto, be my grave,
  "Love yet lives within thy pale,
"Let thy gently rippling wave
  "Giulio's fate alone bewail!"

Thus, in the vision, Giulio sang,—
Then from the azure rock he sprang,
And all is silent, save the moan,
The murmur of the waves alone

* * * * * * * *

* * * * * * * *

Beneath the gay streets, where the light-hearted crowds
  Jest and sing in a fair sunny clime,
Deep beneath is a vault, where oblivion enshrouds
  The condemned who confess not their crime.

---

* A human form in the water of the grotto appears of a silvery hue.

Oh, dark is that dungeon, and dreary, and cold,
    And narrow and noisome each cell,
Oh, countless the tales that those walls could unfold,
    The horrors its chambers could tell!

But foulest of all is one cell, where alone
    Half senseless a murderer lay,
Four slow rolling years had he slept on that stone,
    Till reason and mem'ry have faded away.

Oh, oft on his knees, when imprisoned at first,
    His trial or death he besought,
But no—by the Church is that victim accursed,
    His crime, though confessed, is with sacrilege fraught.*

A monk hath he slain;—and a priest-ruling power
    No justice to such can extend,
Since o'er him the terrors of papacy lower,
    What hope for his torture to end?

---

* By the law of Naples, it is necessary that a criminal should confess before he is executed: it frequently happens, however, that prisoners are, in any case, kept in confinement a long time before they are even tried.

While still, far away on Salerno's fair shores,
    Long fled from her cheeks the bright bloom,
One mourns for the absence of him she deplores;
    Unconscious, untold of his doom.

And day after day, o'er the waters, in vain,
    (Ah! when could such constancy fail?)
Yet hopelessly hoping, her eyes would she strain,
    To catch the first glimpse of his sail.

He comes not—but still her self-flattering heart
    Refuses its anguish to learn,
Nor dares with its long-treasured darling to part,
    The hope of her lost one's return.

Till haply the tale of a peasant she hears,
    How shudd'ring in Naples he'd seen
A wretch who had lain in his dungeon for years
    Led forth to the dread guillotine.

How ghastly and wan, and half fainting, and pale,
    O'ercome with the air long denied,
Yet joyful at last his deliv'rance to hail,
    A Salernian fisherman died.

She hears, and she trembles ; why thus strangely moved
   By the fate of this felon unknown?
Or hast thou, Teresa, the sympathy proved,
   Vouchsafed to true lovers alone?

Howe'er let it be,—from that hour she no more
   Sat vacantly watching the deep,
But the gay laughing boy in his dark face who bore
   The looks of his sire, as now oft she would weep,

Clings closer around her,—his eye, flashing-bright,
   Hath learned o'er her sorrow to cast
A ray of young hope, as a new morning's light
   Breaks in on the shades of the night that is past.

A Lament for Rome.

"Barbarus heu cineres insistet victor et urbem
 Eques sonante verberabit ungulâ."
HORACE, *Epod.* xvi.

"Roma, Roma, non più com' era prima."
National Song.

And is this Rome?* the pow'rful, the sublime,
The sovereign mistress of remotest clime?
This all the record of her might immense,—
All that remains of her magnificence?
Those mould'ring arches, blacken'd columns all,
To witness both her greatness and her fall!—
The voiceless echoes of the silent past,
Sad, solemn relics of an empire vast,

---

* The view from the Capitol of the Forum Romanum, and the few scattered columns and arches which alone remain of all the noble buildings with which it was once surrounded, is strikingly impressive. A desolate, deserted space in the midst of a great city, it offers a melancholy contrast to the bustling scene it must have presented in the days of ancient Rome.

Ye, spared so oft by ruthless fire and sword,
Stupendous fragments, could ye but record
All that your stones have seen; Oh! could ye tell
How Rome, degen'rate, from her glory fell,
How thus disgraced, dishonoured, and profaned,
Till nought but name and ruins have remained;
How that immortal Senate proudly hurled
Laws and submission o'er a prostrate world,
How yon lone Forum, crowded, breathless, hung
On Cicero's thrilling words,—hushed ev'ry tongue,—
How godlike art and golden letters reigned,
And man's philosophy its height attained,
Till listless luxury despised renown,
And tyrants trafficked in the Cæsars' crown.

But ye whose greatness triumphs o'er the grave,
Immortal spirits of the Roman brave,
Whose wisdom, eloquence, will yet inspire
Remotest ages with your sacred fire,
Ye to these crumbling forms, ye still can give
Freshness anew, and bid their mem'ries live.

Who, 'mid the relics of departed life,
Where rest the vot'ries of this world of strife,

Where, in wide vaults, the richly coffined sleep,
Or where the lowly drink oblivion deep,
Shrinks not away and shudders as he feels
The icy languor which around him steals?—
Chill foretaste of the tomb, where, revelling,
Round their dull prey the foul destroyers cling,
Where mightiest monarch must his pride abate,
And reap the knowledge of his loathsome fate.

So thus, where Roman grandeur buried lies,
What startling visions in the spirit rise!
Is this the doom of Empire? this the fate
Of greatness? widow'd of her ancient state,
Cheerless, forlorn, through ages yet to last,
An empty shadow of the vanished past.

My country, Britain! let me turn to thee,
Loved of thy children, fortress of the free;
Shall grim destruction thus thy shores defile,
And fell oppression reach thy favoured isle?
Shall thus thy majesty, dishonoured, weep,
Thy statesmen, warriors, in obstruction* sleep?

* " To lye in cold obstruction."—*Shakspeare.* " In cold obstructtion's apathy." *Byron.*

Here gazing on a 'minished Empire's doom,
Be warned, nor rashly on thy power presume,
Lest pride should steal thy mighty soul away,
And dire corruption plunge thee in decay.

But hark! what greets mine ear? what mocking sound
Disturbs the silence of this hallowed ground?
'T is the shrill bugle, and the measured tread
Of foreign legions;[*] mark them as they thread
With serried ranks yon ruined arches;—ye,
Reared to adorn imperial victory,
Oh! must the Gaul beneath your very shade,
Exulting show what time has Romans made?
The hapless victims of an alien race,
Whose armies revel in their deep disgrace.

O soul-devouring superstition! here
On Bethlehem's simple faith thou dost uprear
A tow'ring pile of falsehood and deceit,
And tramplest truth beneath thine impious feet;
Still must dark error's gloomy clouds obscure
Or quench the light of revelation pure?

[*] The French troops occupying Rome frequently exercise in the *Campo Vaccino*, the site of the ancient Forum. 1857.

A LAMENT FOR ROME.

See, 'mid the Coloseum's crumbling walls,
Whose every stone the birth of truth recalls,
(Oft deeply dyed in hallowed martyr's gore)
False priestcraft rules triumphant as of yore:
'Neath the High Cross,* that stands exalted there,
A mystic band their juggling rites prepare;
With visage veiled they kneel, and loudly pray,
Justice divine by penance to allay,
Invoking aid from countless saints above,
Nor trust the Saviour's all-sufficient love:
Yet, 't is not ours their labours to despise,
'T is God that judges, God that justifies;
Though vain to us should seem their erring prayer,
May not their faith obtain acceptance there?

Rejoice, my spirit, thus withdrawn a space
From weary life, dull labour's dwelling place,
To loftiest heights thy glowing fancy raise,
Inspired with visions of departed days!
Not mine the love of antiquarian lore,
In search of names o'er dusty books to pore,

* Round the Arena of the Coloseum, are placed fourteen small Oratories, and in its centre stands a large wooden cross, before which close-hooded Monks may be frequently seen chanting masses for the dead.

To torture history with a vain surmise,
On every stone some theory to devise;
Go, slave of knowledge, name those columns, say
(With learning deep and wisdom as you may,)*
Why these should *thus* be called, why others fail
To prove the opposite; of what avail?
Rome in her silence is more eloquent
Than all the learning on her ashes spent!
Whether those ruins, held in contest long,
To Pallas, Castor, or to Jove belong,†
Or that sweet fount Egeria's‡ truly be,
They still alike are hallow'd spots to me.

Go, seek th' abode of Cæsar's lofty line,
Yon grass-grown mount, the leafy Palatine;‖

---

* The disputes about the proper designations of numerous ruins have been carried to a great extent of late years, most of the doubtful temples. etc., having been re-christened by the reigning native authority, Il Commendatore Canina.

† The three beautiful Corinthian Columns in the Forum, which have been successively called the Temple of Castor and Pollux, of Jupiter, of Minerva, and lastly, by Canina, the Curia Julia.

‡ The grotto in the Valle Caffarelli, beyond the Porta San Sebastiano, which tradition assigns to Numa's interviews with the nymph Egeria.

‖ The Palatine hill is now covered with vegetation, and only a few shapeless heaps of masonry remain of the celebrated palace of the Cæsars.

Say which the halls where once a glitt'ring crowd
Of mighty princes held their revels proud;
Shew me one trace of great Augustus' throne,
One stone that history may call her own:
Abode of desolation! nought is heard
Save the harsh note of night's ill-omened bird;
O'er shapeless walls the timid lizard creeps,
On crumbling towers the bat his vigil keeps;
A heap of dire confusion! vanish'd all
That could imperial majesty recall.

Yet, fallen Rome, whilst thus I grieve for thee,
Forsaken child of cruel destiny,
Let not my muse those glorious days* forget,
Which shed their lustre on the living yet;
But seek the hill, where frequent grave on grave
Record the valour of thy patriot brave,
Thy last, thy noblest effort to regain
The freedom purchased by thy sires in vain;
On the Janiculum† my footsteps rest,
Where ruined villa, shattered wall attest

* The Revolution of 1848-9, when the Roman Republic bravely defended their city for a considerable period against the French army.

† The French directed their attack on the Janiculum, where the cannonading caused much injury to the villas Doria Pamfili, Quattro Venti and others.

How hotly raged the fierce unequal strife,
How freely Romans gave for Rome their life!
Nor pass unmarked one ever sacred spot,*
In freedom's annals ne'er to be forgot.
Beneath the Vatican's proud walls, behold,
Where deep devotion rivalled deeds of old,
Where arms so feeble could arrest the blow,
And hurl confusion on th' approaching foe.

Oh! may the hopes that triumph brief inspired,
Awake anew, with patriot courage fired,
Stung by their wrongs, uproused, let Romans shew
Souls unsubdued, and tyranny o'erthrow:
To joyful Italy the summons be,
"Arise, oppressed! Rome once again is free!"

* When the French were approaching the city, a few young Romans, dragging a field-piece to a bastion in the gardens of the Vatican which commands the Civita Vecchia road, directed their fire with so murderous an effect, that the enemy were compelled to fall back with considerable loss.

THE EVE OF THE ATTACK.*

Sweeping up the long ravine,
Where our mournful band hath been
   To lay a comrade low,†
Whirling high the piteous dust,
Fiercely roars the savage gust,
   Proud its might to show.

Struggling with the bitter blast,
Every soldier's thought is cast
   On the morrow's fight;—
Shall we rest beneath this hill,
Or our corpses help to fill
   A ghastly trench that night?

* On September 7th, 1855, Sir W. Codrington announced to the Light Division of the Army before Sebastopol the intention of attacking the Great Redan on the morrow. The following lines were suggested by the author's recollections of that momentous evening.

† A private, who had been accidentally killed in camp.

THE EVE OF THE ATTACK.

Shall we, 'scaped the day of strife,
Joying in a rescued life,
   Hold a conquered town,—
Shall we—but we scorn the thought,
Death alone is to be bought,
   If not a victor's crown.

Reaching now the camp, we part,
Each with wild excited heart,
   In sleep our limbs to lay;
Whilst the cannons' constant roll
Speaks to every slumb'rer's soul
   The carnage of the day.

Yet new life in all awoke,
When our chief that ev'ning spoke,
   Bidding us prepare;—
Gladly from the trench-work turned
Ev'ry gallant youth, and burned
   The dire assault to dare.

Long before a city doomed
Had they lain, and scarce entombed
   Countless dying brave;

THE EVE OF THE ATTACK.

Stricken by the murd'rous shell,
Smitten by disease, who fell,
  And found a common grave.

Hast thou viewed a suff'rer languish,
Sinking slow in mortal anguish,
  'Neath thy very eye?
See, within yon fatal line,
England's choicest flowers decline,
  Youth neglected die!

Can ye rest whose hearts of steel
Scorned those hapless ones' appeal,
  Trifling with your trust?
'Midst your lordly grandeur know
All the fearful debt ye owe,
  Treasured in their dust.

Why repeat the oft-told story,
Why tell o'er the dear-bought glory,
  Won upon that shore;
Why recall the hard-fought day,
When our struggles to repay,
  No prize away we bore?

Fruitless all the hopes that rose,
Haunting our dream-tossed repose,
   Through that fevered night;
Ours the doubly galling fate
Rivals' triumph to create,
   Reaping but the fight.

AN EPISODE OF WAR.

"Brief, brave, and glorious was his young career."
                              CHILDE HAROLD, iii. 24.

Oh, hast thou watched a fragile flower,
Child of the sunshine's swift-winged hour,
Just bursting into earliest spring,
Its beauties gently blossoming,
And shedding o'er the peaceful earth
The fragrance of its early birth?
And marked how soon hath drooped its head,
How soon its loveliness hath fled!
How soon the buds, scarce oped in life,
Caught by the raging tempest's strife,
Are scattered far before the wind
And leave a widowed stem behind!
Untimely blasted! over bold,
Too soon it dared the ling'ring cold,—

Snatched from thine eager love away,
The debt of frailness forced to pay!

So fair, so hapless!—he* had grown
The loved of all; though barely shown
To envious Fate, her ruthless wave
O'erwhelmed the hopes his boyhood gave.—
And we were friends in days when beamed
Undimmed life's sunshine, and we dreamed
With sanguine hearts of glory, fame,
The honour of a soldier's name,
The pride of valour, and of all
The deep delusions which appal
The worn-out wand'rer who has sought
Each in its turn, and found it nought.

Who, wearied with the selfish war,
The harsh unsympathizing jar
Of worldly feelings, would not give
All he has won in life to live
Yet once again the winsome years
Of boyish hopes, and boyish fears;

* A young officer of the 30th Regiment, well known to the author, and of great promise, who was killed at the assault of the Redan Fort, Sebastopol, September 8th, 1855.

To breathe once more the bracing air
Of early hope, of hours when care,
Engendered fresh at every birth,
Fled far before our careless mirth!
Such were we, when our youthful thought,
Wildly enthusiastic, caught
The love of martial deeds—'t was then,
Just rising, as we deemed, to men,
We marked the trumpet's thrilling note
Sound for the fight, and proudly float,
Long-furled in peaceful folds at rest,
Allied the Standards of the West.
We parted; 't was the earliest woe
Our friendship had been doomed to know;
Still hoping, on the eastern shore,
Where now the tide of battle bore
Our country's hosts, again to tell
The school-day triumphs treasured well;
Again, in sterner scenes, to seek
The mem'ries of each boyish freak,
And mingle in the future's store
The sweetness of our days of yore.

The morn is gloomy; like a pall
Still o'er the Camp the night-mists fall,
And veil the barren hills which frown
On Balaklava's distant town.
Not long hath dawned the light of day,
When issue forth a long array
Of men whose faded garments, torn
In many a shred, and features worn
Attest how, weary night on night,
Spared by the deadly missiles' flight,
They lay unmurm'ring in the trench,
Whilst now their ranks the storm-clouds drench.
And now the frost-bound icy air
Thrills death-like through the stoutest there.
Yet, dauntless still, with many a jest,
(Though bound for murd'rous work confest)
Down marched they, confident of fate,
The signal of attack to wait.

Not long we stayed; with whirling head,
Lost in excitement, onward sped,
'Mid shot and shells' unceasing fire,
Our weakened column;—mounting higher,

Whilst at each footstep fell a man,
We pressed within the Great Redan,
And then a fearful pause!

Deaf'ning the roar; and yet a cheer
In well-known accents reached mine ear,
And as the iron storm he braved,
And on his sword his cap he waved,
To animate his falt'ring band,
Breathless with zeal, one grasped my hand;
" Oh, strange, oh, passing strange, to meet
In such a scene, and first* to greet
Thee *thus*," I cried; he scarcely spoke,
But from his eye a lustre broke,
Whilst onward still he strove in vain
The gory summit to attain:—
No more I saw him, like a star,
Shot through the orbs of heav'n afar,
He passed, and vanished from my sight,
Lost in the thick'ning maze of fight.

---

* He had only landed a few days before in the Crimea, and this was the first occasion on which he had been under fire, or had been seen by the author, their regiments being encamped at some distance from each other.

'T is evening ;—with the din subside
Our wild emotions, and the tide
Of feeling, rushing back, o'erflows,
While deeper ev'ry instant grows
Dark sorrow's heart-enthralling shade,
As in the dull cold earth we laid
Forms which but yesterday were filled
With brimming mirth for ever stilled ;
And mine to hear a tale, my heart,
Unwilling though from hope to part,
Already told,—how, 'mid the foe,
Yet warm with young devotion's glow,
Smiling in death, his lifeless clay
Unburied on the rampart lay.

QUEEN VICTORIA'S FAREWELL TO THE BALTIC FLEET.*

Proud heave thou, mighty glitt'ring tide,
On whose bright bosom stately ride
   The flower of Albion's peerless fleet;
Entrusted to thy surging wave
A noble fleet of warriors brave,
   For glorious death or victory meet.

Still prouder heave—more glitt'ring shine,
A nobler burden still is thine,
   A British Sovereign in her pride,—
For mark, amid yon mighty throng
Of tow'ring masts, and bulwarks strong.
   A " Fairy" bark majestic glide.

As when, in Britain's early day,
'Gainst the rude spoiler's tyrant sway,
   The Warrior Queen her legions led,

---

* Composed on the subject " Regina classi ad bellum proficiscenti valedicit."—*Ex. Coll., Oxford, May*, 1854.

Thus, at Victoria's just behest,
Their ancient zeal her sons attest
   In freedom's cause their blood to shed.

" Farewell," she cries; " in such a cause,
Breathes there a Briton who could pause
   To lay his long-sheath'd weapon bare ?
Go, to the world our prowess prove,
Deep-treasured in your monarch's love,
   And hallowed by your country's prayer."

A mighty shout bursts from that host,
Far echoing o'er the peaceful coast;
   Then loud the cannon's thunders roll :—
Whilst each rough sailor's gaze intent
Upon his Sovereign's form is bent,
   And loyal ardour thrills his soul.

Thus Britain proud defiance hurls,
Again her dauntless flag unfurls,
   And shrill the trumpet's war notes swell :-
On Eastern shores her banners wave,
Far northern seas her vessels lave,
   Aggression's insolence to quell.

TO THE VALE OF RYDAL.

A wand'rer in a foreign clime
Where art and nature soar sublime;
On Alpine heights enwrapp'd in snows,
Where the loud torrent foaming flows;
Through Italy's vine-trellised plains,
'Neath buried ages' vast remains,
I wended my delighted way;
Lingering for many a too-brief day
At wisdom's shrine, where poet's song
Hath breathed on nature, where belong
The very stones and dust to fame,
She, who from chaos can reclaim
The meanest relics of the past,
And round them robes of splendour cast.

Now, bosom'd in the wooded hills,
Laved by a hundred bubbling rills,
A woodland valley, loved of yore,
Invites me to repose once more;—

TO THE VALE OF RYDAL.

No boast is thine of mighty deeds,
Blood hath not stained thy dewy meads,
But nature here hath raised a throne,
Crown'd with a beauty all her own.—
Here nature's poet* sweetness drew,
Learning his mountain muse to woo,
And shed upon his simple lay
A charm no time can tear away.—
Rydal, thy heights with Alps compared
Are lowly mounds,—of verdure bared
No tow'ring rocks are thine, nor know
Thy glades the mighty curse of snow,
The thund'ring avalanche—'t is thine
To charm the eye with grace divine,
Weaving around the willing heart
A love no grandeur can impart.

Thy Lake, outspread in calm repose,
Traced on its bosom, softly shows
The craggy rock, and leafy height,
The guardians of its waters bright;

Wordsworth was an ardent admirer of the scenery immediately
nd his secluded abode.

TO THE VALE OF RYDAL.

Calm as an infant's breast, no wave
Ruffles the surface, nothing save
The heron's* cry is heard, awhile
She soars above her shelt'ring isle,
Those mossy crags where the young brood
Luxuriate in solitude;
Where, as a king, the noble bird
Rules undisturb'd—no step is heard;
The grasp of man, the common lot
Of nature, spares this favour'd spot.

When o'er the valley rapid fly
The fleecy wand'rers of the sky,
When Loughrigg's† steeps now wrapp'd in shade,
Now bathed in sunshine, glow and fade,
When the rich tints of Autumn morn
The ever varying woods adorn,
Then, Rydal, thou may'st yield to none,
Sweetest of vales; no southern sun

---

* On the small mere of Rydal are several picturesque islets, on the largest of which is one of the few heronries now remaining in England:—the noble birds are allowed undisturbed possession of the spot by the laudable care of Lady Le Fleming, to whom the lake belongs.

† A rocky hill bounding on one side the narrow valley of Rydal.

Beams on a brighter scene than thine,
Nor lights a beauty more divine.
Thou little streamlet,* ever flowing,
Brawling and bubbling, onward going;
Now, with resistless headlong force,
Sweeps on thy water's wintry course,—
Now, slowly purling 'midst the stones,
Low murm'ring thine untutored tones,
Still onward in the sweet spring tide
Thy 'minish'd currents gently glide;—
And yet thou art the same, unchanged
By changeful years, whilst I have ranged
O'er earth and sea, since, when a child,
Thy voice my youthful heart beguiled,
Since when, up grown, again I sought,
Time after time, thy banks, and caught
The feeling of the landscape blending
All beauties, and thy waters lending
Activity and life to all;—
Thus, Rothay, doth thy sound recall
All that is loveliest in my life,
Days yet untouched by toil and strife,

---

* A remarkably clear and picturesque stream flowing through Grasmere and Rydal Lakes into Windermere.

Yet breathing innocence and joy,
Ere time could canker and destroy.
And ye, loved friends, whose happy fate
In this bright valley to await
Joys brighter yet—ye, too, the same,
The warmest tribute ever claim
Of my heart's pure affection, ye,
Endeared from earliest years to me,
Whose words and works recorded are
In realms above; no silv'ry star
Shines brighter 'mid the shades of night,
Than round ye beams religion's light;
Here, in your calm retreat, ye give
Your hearts to heaven, and learn to live
Amid the sweetest scenes of time
As those who seek a fairer clime,
Which, when these fading days have past,
And earth has crumbled, yet shall last;—
When from on high destruction hurled
Dissolves in space the crashing world,
Virtue immortal shall arise
To reap the bliss that time denies.

SONNETS.

DISAPPOINTMENT.

Say, fell betrayer of the hopeful heart,
Why thus the fancied images we deem
Bright, while remote, as poet's airy dream,
In stern reality must ever part,
Quelled by the poison of thy 'venomed dart,
With half their loveliness; ne'er to redeem
The promised splendour that withal they teem,—
Deeply delusive as the painter's art.—
Oh! how thy touch my spirit low hath bowed,
Dread disappointment, o'er the joyous flame
That burned within hath swept a sudden cloud,
As with a bitter warning to proclaim
The doom of all things, and the common shroud
To fold in endless night hope, love, and fame.

II.

HOPE.

Undying solace of our mortal lot,
Bestowed from high in pitying mercy pure
From dark despair our sorrow to secure,—
When in the grave of Time the world shall rot,
Its woe and happiness alike forgot,
Calmly triumphant shalt thou yet endure,
Till ripe eternity thy sons assure
Of heavenly joys that here they doubted not.
Thou Stay of Life, an angel brighter far
Than man deserves his wandered way to cheer,
Bright as to sea-tossed mariner the star
Which shews the track his shattered bark would steer,
Amid the rocks its heavenward course that mar
Doth to the soul thy beacon fire appear.

III.

MELANCHOLY.

Oh, strangely welcome oft to me thy shade
In hours of solitude that give repose
From life's stern conflict!—As the blast o'erthrows
The budding verdure of the leafy glade,
And in the havoc of its splendour made,
The frailness of our much-loved nature shows,
As if a silent token to disclose
How soon in dust all beauty must be laid;
So when regret hath quenched my gushing mirth,
And hope declines in apathy's dull night,
Withdrawn awhile from ev'ry tie of earth,
I view its treasures in their truest light;
Phantoms of joy, impatient from their birth
Swift from our grasp to wing their eager flight.

IV.

CONTENTMENT.

Contentment, Eldorado of a life!
Pure fountain of the only earthly joy
Whose sweets can never on its vot'ries cloy!
When proud ambition, in its selfish strife,
Severs the heart, as with a ruthless knife,
From kindly sympathies, a base alloy
Will oft the value of the prize destroy,
And render greatness with unquiet rife.
See to the mountain-shadowed, humble cot,
Nestling apart in modest solitude,
Contentment, as enamoured of the spot,
Fly from the great to seek a shelter rude;
And happiness her priceless gifts allot,
Long by the rich in fruitless off'rings wooed.

MYSTERY.

When men the mighty marvels that surround
And glorify the world would closely scan,
And trace in all the structure and the plan,
Though science stretch her utmost power to sound
The hidden causes, yet there still is found
In each a barrier, which the mind of man
Dares not to pierce,—in vain, since time began
Searching the depths that in itself abound.—
Yet firmly planted in the mystic soul
The love of myst'ry;—impulse undefined
Prompts it to linger where obscurest roll
The clouds of doubt, and, reason left behind,
To soar through trackless realms without control,
On fancy borne, false as the fickle wind.

VI.

AFFECTION.

As to some time-worn tree the tender shoot,
The twig of clust'ring ivy closely clings,
So round a weary heart affection flings
Its warm embrace, and cherishes the fruit
Of new-born sympathy; its firm-fix'd root
Puts forth fresh branches every year that brings
Decay to life, while on his restless wings
Time hovers nearer with a warning mute.—
Endearing solace! who would madly strive
To court their happiness without thine aid?
Vain, bright-eyed pleasure opes her luscious hive
Of teeming sweets—vain, every wish obey'd,
Alone, unloved, in lux'ry's depth they dive,
To find for ever longings unallayed.

SONG.

Bright sparkling goddess of our mirth,
   Sweet mourner in our grief,
The gayest elf that lives on earth,
   Yet sad beyond belief,—
           Fairy Music!

Now in the lightsome, careless dance
   Thy silv'ry echoes ring,
And o'er the hours that swiftly glance
   A soft enchantment fling,—
           Merry Music!

Now, to the tales of love and war
   A magic canst thou give,
And waft them on thy strains afar
   On every lip to live,—
           Thrilling Music!

Oft when distills the bitter tear,
   When pleasures die around,
Then, welcome to the wearied ear
   Thy sweetly plaintive sound,—
           Solemn Music!

For art thou not a heaven-born gift,
   That angels love to share,—
Thy mission *Here* our souls to lift
   To perfect concord *There*,—
           Holy Music?

CONSTANCY.

Ne'er could the youthful eager vow
    So firm our hearts have twined,
Did not mature affection now
    Their steady union bind.

Oh, deep-deceived, too oft, are they,
    Whose love to life hath sprung
All perfect in the magic day,
    By many a minstrel sung.

Too swiftly born! 't will swiftly die,
    Unnurtured and unblest;
Wounded by treach'rous Time, 't will fly
    The chilled and wearied breast.

Thou, Constancy, the healthful child
    Of early hopes and fears,—
A golden prize, which ne'er beguiled
    The love that feeds on years.

TO A YOUNG LADY ON HER BIRTHDAY.

Though lower above us wintry skies,
And icy cold pervades the frame,
Yet let my willing muse arise,
To sing of sunshine e'er the same.

No dark'ning cloud can yet obscure
The brightness of thy youthful heart,
And nought can to thy spirit pure
But happiness and joy impart.

Oh, "sweet sixteen!" most charming age
Entranced with brimming joy and bliss,
May'st thou ne'er look on mem'ry's page
And sigh for such a day as this!

The world its countless treasures fair,
Holds forth to tempt thee, beauteous maid
But may'st thou choose with anxious care
The gems whose lustre ne'er can fade.

This tribute of my love for thee
Most willingly I haste to pay,
And that thy lot may happy be
Is the fond prayer of this my lay.

THOSE EYES OF THINE!

Those eyes of thine! that darkly show
The current of thine inmost thought,
Now softly melt, now brightly glow,
With ev'ry changing feeling fraught.

Those eyes of thine! that o'er me shed
A fascination wild and deep,
Each waking thought a captive led,
And haunted e'en the hours of sleep.

Still do they seem my love to claim,
Now that, united heart to heart,
I call thee by a fonder name,
And know that we no more may part.

ODE TO "THE DERBY."[*]

"Sunt quos curriculo pulverem Olympicum
Collegisse juvat."—
Horace, Carm. i. 1

I.

Who shall describe the tumult loud,
The bustle of the motley crowd,
Who madly rush into the train,
Heedless alike of cold and rain,
For Epsom bound, one noted day,
In chilly, wat'ry, English May?
Maius, thou pride of springtide rosy,
Month of the poets, and the prosy,
Of concert, opera, and ball,
And meetings pious in a certain hall!

---

[*] Suggested by "the Derby" of 1858, which occurred during the memorable debate on Lord Derby's Indian policy.

II.

But yet, in these degen'rate days,
When ruthless steam and iron ways
Have banished to their long abode
The ancient glories of the road,
Tradition will assert his sway,
Triumphant, on the Derby day;
And vehicles, for months that rust,
Again emerge to court the dust;
And " swells" still vote the train a " bore,"
To wield the long-dishonoured whip once more.

III.

Still, 'mid a storm of glorious " chaff,"
On lofty drags their champagne quaff
The " nobby" patrons of the ring—
Still, in the dust their ditties sing
The real legless British tars,
Survivors of a hundred wars,—
Still, in conveyance undefined,
Crammed close within, before, behind,
Gents of untold-of shape and sort,
Display their talent for impromptu sport.

IV.

Behold the varied Epsom Down,
Now graced by the " élite " of Town,
From noble lord and wise M.P.,
And Sprig of Aristocracy,
To "turfites" of the "knowing" stamp,
Suggestive of the British Scamp;—
Moustachioed Guards, of awful mien,
Enhance the splendour of the scene;
The Blues, the Coldstreams, and no lack
Of others, unattached,—yclept the Black.

V.

Oh, dense and diverse is the throng,
Whose glories to the day belong!
Here banjos, pipes, and organs thrill
The mortal ear with music shrill,—
Here genuine sons of nigger races
Display their cork be-blackened faces,—
Here, acrobats afford the treat
Of seeing heads where should be feet,
And babes who barely walk alone,
Evince a strange deficiency of bone.

VI.

Sharpers and thimble-rigs (of course)
Muster in overwhelming force;
And cheats of various grade and style
The verdant of their " brass" beguile;—
And wise Egyptia's tawny maid
Pursues her old prophetic trade,
Wedding fair girls—(the money down)—
To dukes and lords for half a crown,—
While blushes, titt'rings, glances sly,
Enchant the swain who—carves the luncheon pie.

VII.

But shall my muse presume to sing
The marvels of the mystic " ring?"
Where " odds" are all, and all are odd,
A volume in each wink and nod;
No need of equine knowledge now,—
To know a racer from a cow;—
Proficient on the " turf" to be,
" Bookmaking," " hedging," £. s. d.,
Form the chief studies now required,
When " artful dodging" is so much admired.

VIII.

Thou dweller on the banks of Thames,
Who yearly, at the springs of Ems,
At Baden, Homburg, or Wiesbaden,
Behold'st the gambler's features harden,
As from the board he sweeps the cash,—
Forbear to boast in accents rash
The virtues of thy native land,
Lest, the next Derby, 'neath the " Stand,"
A German, 'midst that cream of scenes,
Should gravely ask you what—" *ein blackleg*" means.

IX.

Yet who in London can keep quiet
When Parliament itself runs riot?
Cuts short the business of the nation,
And votes debate a " botheration ! "
While, in the bracing Epsom airs,
Statesmen relax the weighty cares
Of striving hard, in either case,
To gain, or not to lose, a place ;
In speeches for their country's weal,
Their own peculiar talents to reveal.

X.

Should e'en a contest fierce be raging,
And every member's soul engaging,
A faction fight, of moment great,
Big with a ministerial fate,
One which precludes, when once begun,
All chance of getting *business* done,
Still deadly foes in mid career
Stop short, and poise the fatal spear,—
Forth from the " House" to Epsom burst,
To see which thorough-bred will come in first.

XI.

"They're off! they're off!" "Aye, there they go!"
" Bravo the pink!—he has it." No!
Swift as a lightning flash, they pass
In one confused bright-coloured mass,—
Swelling yet louder and more loud
The shouts of the excited crowd,
Till by the Post the foremost run,
One "length" apart;—"the Derby" 's won!—
Hurrah!—and may the day afar be
When we shall celebrate the final " Derby!"

THE NOVEL AND THE STAGE.

A VISION OF THE PRESENT.*

"They are the abstract and brief chronicles of the time."
Hamlet.

"I come not to offend,
But with good will."
Midsummer Night's Dream.

I.

The other ev'ning when I 'd read
The pond'rous "Times," my thoughts were led
    Within a "study brown;"
I 'd waded through a long "critique"
Upon the novel of the week,
    And, as I laid it down,

II.

I wondered at the lavish praise
Of what, in these fast going days,
    Would pass for sentiment,—
Of Fiction's half-religious school,
Pathetically worked by rule,
    And dexterously bent

* January, 1859.

III.

To humour the young lady's taste,
And cause her on its page to waste
    One half, at least, her day;
Drinking with eager eye the sweets
Of pathos in each line she meets,
    Jostling upon the way.

IV.

Yet whilst good "Amy" and her "Heirs"
Enchant our fair ones, unawares
    Within their circle stealing,
An artful renegade, whose style,
Tender of tend'rest, can beguile
    The most correct in feeling,

V.

Finds in the drawing-room oft a place,
Where scarce he'd dare to show his face,
    E'en in so bright a binding,
Divested of the borrowed plumes,
And air of virtue he assumes,
    The sober critic blinding.

VI.

I 've lately seen a fast young " Guy"
The morals of the age defy,
    And boast a dubious creed,
Which should secure his leaves a home
Where the long-shelved and shabby tome
    Of Fielding runs to seed.

VII.

" But he 's such fun ! we must forget
His little faults : the naughty pet
    Has run through two editions ; "
Age of the strict and pious ! Well
May future generations tell
    With wonder your transitions

VIII.

From " Social Evil" Meetings vast,
And " Refuges," and trumpet-blast
    Of Charity quite dinning,
To doubtful Novel and Report
Of curious cases in the Court
    Of Matrimonial sinning.

IX.

But we're improving! Never mind,—
We've left our Fathers far behind,
  To woo a prospect *Bright*
Of reformation on a scale
To make the purse-proud peerage quail,
  And shortly set a light

X.

To palace and to feudal hall,
And throw oblivion over all
  Regard for rank and birth;
And bring us down to what we are,—
"Shop-keeping" mortals, who should war
  Alone on cotton's worth.

XI.

But I'm digressing; and, I fear,
Have scarcely managed to keep clear
  Of politics; but yet,
In pity, sage Reformer, skip
Those two last stanzas, and the shp
  Of tell-tale pen forget.

XII.

I wished to talk of Literature,—
If such a thing will then endure
    'Midst all things transformation,—
And mention one or two whose fame,
Founded on genius, yet may claim
    Some slight consideration.

XIII.

For fiction still a gifted few
Can boast, amid the motley crew
    Who scribble for the " Row :"—
Though some have been content to part
With half the humour and the art
    Their first productions show.

XIV.

How far beneath the master touch
Of " Pickwick," " Boz," and " Dombey," such
    A tale as " Little Dorrit !"
'T is Dickens ;—so we all must read,
To vote it very *slow* indeed,
    And grudge the money for it.

XV.

And you, who aimed your shafts at " Vánity,"
And trampled on the world's urbánity,
    Though nothing can abate your
Contempt for Women, " Snobs," and " Georges,"
With weakened force your pen disgorges
    Its spite of human nature.

XVI.

Rise, Bulwer; leave Colonial cares
To those who thrive upon the airs
    Of office and dispute;
And let thy talents once again
Invigorate thy graphic strain,
    And wake the music mute,

XVII.

Which murmured through " Zanoni's" page,
And from the depths of classic age
    Pompeii's beauties drew:
Re-seek the power that dignified
Rome's patriot son, who vainly tried
    To rouse her fame anew.

XVIII.

Where 's Tancred?—hard at crabbéd figures!
Emancipating Jews and Niggers;
    As Horace told Mæcenas,
In sob'rest prose he must (proud fate!)
The Wars of—Debt and Credit state,
    And from his novels wean us.

XIX.

Oh fallen Thespis! once the wit
Scorned not to patronize the pit,
    And give to worth applause;
Now, from the Continent imported,
A vapid Comedy, distorted,
    The gaping Cockney draws.

XX.

Is native talent swept away?
Far from it, but it does not "pay,"
    Save when it turns grotesque,
With meanest jest and silliest pun,
Twists genius into wretched fun,
    The play-bills call Burlesque.

XXI.

Shakspeare, 't is true, from slumbers long
Sometimes awakes, but then a throng
    Of ballet-girls surround;
In Dress and Scen'ry quite sublime,
Upholst'ry, Music, Pantomime,
    His homely voice is drowned.

XXII.

Italian Opera 's all the fashion,—
Alboni's notes, Gardoni's passion,
    Titiens' harmonious sob!
While dinners not till half-past eight
Complete the Drama's piteous fate,
    And hand her to the mob.

ERRATA.

Page 1, for " Heroid, Ep. v." *read* Heroid. Ep. v.
,, 3, line 6, for "joyous" *read* buoyant.
,, 9, line 9, for " shadows," *read* shadows;
,, 16, lines 11 and 13, *insert* a comma after "darkest" and after " spot "
,, 35, for " Childe Harold, iii. 24," *read* Childe Harold, iii. 57.
,, 45, line 13, *insert* a comma after " steeps "

XXI.

Shakspeare, 't is true, from slumbers long
Sometimes awakes, but then a throng
　　Of ballet-girls surround ;
In Dress and Scen'ry quite sublime,

WS - #0055 - 300623 - C0 - 229/152/5 - PB - 9781330746455 - Gloss Lamination